This notebook belongs to:

____________________________

Made in the USA
Middletown, DE
16 December 2019

80831435R00062